meal in a bowl

RYLAND
PETERS
& SMALL

meal
in a bowl

Elsa Petersen-Schepelern

photography by Jeremy Hopley

Designer **Paul Tilby**
Editor **Elsa Petersen-Schepelern**
Creative Director **Jacqui Small**
Publishing Director **Anne Ryland**
Production **Meryl Silbert**
Food Stylist **Melina Keays**
Stylist **Page Marchese**
Photographer's Assistant **Catherine Rowlands**
Author Photograph **Francis Loney**

Acknowledgements
My thanks to my sister Kirsten, Luc Votan, Peter
Bray, Clare Ferguson, Sonia Stevenson, Nowelle
and Clemente Valentino-Capezza, Susan, and Tim.
Thanks to Becky Johnson for her enthusiastic
and knowledgeable assistance and for helping
with recipe testing—and to the shoot team who
made the whole experience such fun.
My heartfelt thanks also to the ceramicists and
suppliers who lent us the beautiful bowls for
this book, including Egg, Livingstone Studio,
Oggetti, Maryse Boxer, Muji, Sue Paraskeva,
and Divertimenti.

Notes
All spoon measurements are level unless
otherwise noted.
Ovens should be preheated to the specified
temperature. If using a convection oven,
cooking times should be reduced according
to the manufacturer's instructions.

First published in 1998, reprinted in 2000, by
Ryland Peters & Small, Inc.,
150 West 56th Street, Suite 6303,
New York, N.Y. 10019

10 9 8 7 6 5 4 3 2

Text © Elsa Petersen-Schepelern 1998
Design and photographs
© Ryland Peters & Small 1998

Printed and bound in China by
Toppan Printing Co.

ISBN 1-84172-070-4

A CIP catalog record for this book is available
from the Library of Congress.

contents

introduction

These thirty recipes are just a few of my favorite casual dishes. I cook them as a quick meal-in-a-bowl when I'm by myself, or in larger quantities when friends and colleagues drop over for a casual lunch or dinner. If you increase the quantities, many of these dishes can be prepared in bulk for parties, when people need a little sustenance to help the conversation swing. In fact, they're so versatile I also find they can be adapted for more formal occasions—the sort of dinner party when I'm playing ladies! The only difference is that the bowls need to be a little more formal than for the more casual "dinner-in-front-of-the-fire" kind of event.

Every cuisine seems to have dishes suitable for the Meal in a Bowl treatment. My own passions are for fresh-tasting Asian dishes, just packed with spice and flavor—and for comforting European food from the "Cuisine Grandmere" school of thought.

Choose the size of bowl that suits your appetite—mine is enormous in winter and only a little less enthusiastic in summer. You'll soon find which of these categories applies to you. Be assured, these recipes are not for birdlike appetites!

singapore laksa

Laksas are found in different forms all over the Malay peninsula. In Penang they are almost overpoweringly fishy, while in Singapore they can be very spicy—this version is milder. You can vary the ingredients according to what's available in the market, and to suit your own taste: but the basics should be a truly wonderful, flavorful stock, plus noodles. I like Japanese somen noodles, but fine cellophane noodles are probably more common. The spice paste can also be simplified by using one of the ready-made Thai pastes instead.

2 tablespoons corn or peanut oil

2 cups coconut milk

2 cups boiling fish or chicken stock

1 cooked chicken breast, shredded

2 fried Chinese fishcakes, sliced (optional)

12 uncooked shrimp (optional)

7 oz. somen or cellophane noodles, soaked according to package instructions

6 scallions

1 bunch of cilantro

4 handfuls of beansprouts, trimmed

1 bunch of mint or Vietnamese mint

spice paste

3 stalks lemongrass, sliced

4 garlic cloves, sliced

1 inch fresh ginger, peeled and sliced

3 shallots or 6 Thai shallots, chopped

4 candlenuts or 8 blanched almonds

3 red chiles, seeded

1 teaspoon turmeric

1 teaspoon salt

1 teaspoon sugar, preferably brown

serves 4

Grind all the spice paste ingredients in a spice grinder or blender, adding a little oil if necessary. Heat the oil in a wok and stir-fry the paste for 6 to 8 minutes without burning. Add the coconut milk and stock and simmer gently for 5 minutes to develop the flavors. Add the chicken, fishcakes, and shrimp, if using, and simmer for 2 minutes or until the shrimp become opaque. Prepare the noodles according to the package instructions. Share the noodles, chicken, fishcakes, shrimp, scallions, cilantro, beansprouts, and mint between 4 big bowls. Pour over the coconut stock and serve.

soups

thai mussel soup

with coconut milk and lemongrass

A Thai version of the French classic, moules à la marinière. Most mussels sold in shops have been farmed, and seem to need less cleaning than wild ones. In any case, you should scrub the shells with a small brush and either pull off or cut off the "beards." Use mussels that are tightly closed —tap any open ones against your worktop, and discard them if they still don't close. Steam the mussels open, discarding any that stay closed. When you buy mussels, keep them cool and use them the same day. The best mussel-eating implement is an empty pair of shells—use them as pincers to nip the others out of their shells.

To make the coconut stock, put the lemongrass, ginger, lime leaves, and garlic in a small food processor and work to a smooth paste. Heat the oil in a saucepan, add the paste and chiles, and stir-fry until you cough. Add the fish stock, bring to a boil, and simmer 5 to 10 minutes to extract the flavors. Add the coconut milk and heat to simmering.

Chop 1 stalk of lemongrass into a large saucepan with the fish stock or water and boil briskly. Add the mussels, one layer at a time, and cook until they open, transferring them to 4 big bowls as they do.

Strain the coconut stock over the mussels. Sprinkle with sliced chiles, lime zest, and cilantro and serve immediately, with another empty bowl to take the discarded shells.

Be prepared to double the quantity of mussels because your guests will love this dish!

1 stalk lemongrass

1 cup fish stock or water

2–3 bags mussels, about 2 lb. each

coconut stock

3 stalks lemongrass, chopped

1 inch fresh ginger, peeled and sliced

6 kaffir lime leaves, snipped

3 garlic cloves, sliced

1–2 tablespoons corn oil

1–2 red chiles, sliced

2 cups fish stock

2 cups coconut milk

to serve

2 red chiles, finely sliced

grated zest of 3 kaffir limes

sprigs of cilantro

serves 4

chinese treasure soup

I always buy Chinese barbecued duck and pork, but you can make your own by rubbing with chile oil or honey and 5-spice, then roasting or broiling. Other treasures can be added to taste, including wontons of ground pork, fish balls or pork balls, and other Chinese vegetables such as bok choy, pea shoots, lotus root, and bamboo shoots. The usual number of treasures is the magical eight.

Heat the barbecued duck and barbecued pork in the oven at 400°F until hot. (If cooking your own duck or pork, see the note below.)

To make the wontons, mix the ground pork, bamboo shoots, and salt in a bowl. Put 1 tablespoon of mixture in the middle of each wonton skin and brush a circle of egg white around it. Twirl the wonton skin around the filling to make a shuttlecock shape.

Put all the stock ingredients in a saucepan and simmer for 30 minutes to meld the flavors. Strain out the solids and return the stock to the rinsed pan. Return the stock to a boil and add the carrot and wontons. Simmer for 3 to 5 minutes until the wontons rise to the surface and the filling is cooked.

Put the shrimp, beancurd, cabbage, and wontons in 4 big bowls, then pour over the boiling stock. Add the beansprouts, shredded duck, and pork, and serve with chopsticks and Chinese spoons.

Note: If using char-grilled duck, rub 1 duck breast with 5-spice powder and honey. Heat a stove-top grill-pan and cook, skin side down, until the fat begins to run. Pour off the fat at intervals, and continue cooking for about 20 minutes until the skin is crispy. Turn it over and cook the other side until brown—the center will remain pink. Set aside to set the juices then cut crosswise into ½-inch slices.

To cook your own pork, brush with chile oil and roast at 475°F until very crisp. Set aside to set the juices, then slice into bite-sized pieces.

½ **Chinese barbecued duck, shredded**

1 piece of Chinese barbecued pork spareribs, about 6 inches square, chopped into bite-sized pieces (optional)

1 carrot, scored lengthwise, then finely sliced

6 uncooked shrimp, shelled but with tail fins intact

2 sticks fried beancurd, sliced

2 leaves Chinese cabbage, sliced

a handful of fresh beansprouts, trimmed

wontons

1 cup ground pork

3 canned bamboo shoots, chopped

a pinch of salt

12 wonton skins

1 egg white, beaten

chinese stock

8 cups chicken stock

4 star anise

4 inches fresh ginger, peeled and finely sliced

1 onion, sliced

serves 4

Japanese noodle soups are amazingly quick and easy. The smoked fish used here can be replaced by any number of other ingredients, such as cooked chicken, barbecued pork, finely sliced beef, or blanched vegetables. Just make sure the pieces are bite-sized for easy chopstick-wielding. Dashi, the delicious Japanese stock that smells of the sea, is made from seaweed and minced bonito, a species of tuna, and sold as powder or liquid concentrate in some of the larger supermarkets, as well as Asian shops.

japanese noodle soup

with seaweed and smoked fish

2 packets Japanese noodles (udon, ramen, somen, or soba)

1 lb. smoked haddock or cod, skinned and cut in 4 squares

4 cups dashi stock (see recipe introduction)

1 small package dried wakame seaweed (optional)

4 scallions, finely sliced diagonally

Japanese 7-spice powder—*shichimi togarishi* (optional)

to serve

wasabi paste

Japanese soy sauce

serves 4

Prepare the noodles according to the package instructions. Drain, then put into cold water.

Put the fish in a bowl, then pour over boiling water. Leave for 2 minutes, then drain (if you like, the liquid may be used to make the stock, but the stock will then be a little cloudy.)

Heat the stock, add the wakame seaweed, reheat to boiling, then add the fish and drained noodles and reheat to boiling point.

Serve immediately, sprinkled with the sliced scallions and Japanese 7-spice powder, if using. Serve separate small dishes of wasabi paste and another of soy sauce.

pho bo—vietnamese beef noodle soup

2 packages fresh *ho-fun* noodles or 4 bundles dried *banh pho* broad rice noodles

1 onion, finely sliced

1–4 hot red chiles, seeded and finely sliced

4 oz. rump or fillet steak, very finely sliced (freezing it first makes it easier to slice)

2 tablespoons lime or lemon juice

1 bunch of fresh cilantro

1 bunch of Vietnamese basil, sliced (do not use European—omit if you can't find Asian)

1 bunch of Vietnamese mint

1 lime, quartered

⅓ cup *nuoc mam* (Vietnamese fish sauce), to serve

Vietnamese beef stock

3 quarts beef stock

3–4 onions, finely sliced

1 inch fresh ginger, sliced

8 star anise

½ lemon or lime, with rind

1 tablespoon fish sauce

1 teaspoon sugar

serves 4

My Vietnamese nephew is, I'm irritated to have to admit, the very best cook in our family. He moved to Australia as a student, and had to learn to cook very fast indeed. He has contributed many breathtakingly wonderful dishes to our family repertoire, and this is just one of them. In Vietnam, salt is not served at the table, so all dishes must be seasoned as they are being cooked. Luc uses fresh ho-fun noodles, sold folded into book-sized packs, soft, moist, and ready to use. Mostly they are sold ready-cut: if not, cut them into ½-inch strips. If you want to make the beef stock from scratch, use 4 lb. beef bones and 1½ lb. stewing steak and simmer with the onions and spices for about 4 hours. I'm lazy, so I give the easier cheat's method!

First flavor the beef stock by simmering it in a saucepan with the remaining stock ingredients for about 15 minutes. If using dried noodles, put them into a bowl and cover with hot water. Let soak for 30 minutes, then refresh in cold water. Leave in cold water until ready to serve. If using ho-fun noodles, carefully cut or separate them into strips.

Simmer the onion in boiling water for 2 minutes (or microwave for 2 minutes.) Dip the noodles briefly in boiling water until hot, then divide between 4 big bowls. Add the onions and chiles, then the beef on top. Pour over the boiling stock, then add the lemon or lime juice and herbs. Serve with wedges of lime, a separate bowl of nuoc mam (Vietnamese fish sauce—you can use Thai instead if you like,) chopsticks, and a optional tablespoon so you don't slurp too loudly!

Two classic Tuscan soups for the price of one recipe—serve it the day it's made, or the next day after reboiling—"ribollita." The lettuce added at the end isn't traditional, but I like the extra crunch!

tuscan ribollita

Soak the beans 4 to 6 hours in cold water to cover. Drain, then put into a saucepan with the onion wedges, quartered carrot, and half the garlic. Cover with water, bring to a boil, and simmer until done (the time will depend on the age of the beans, but reckon on about 1 hour.)

Drain and remove the flavorings, then put half the beans in a food processor and work to a rough purée. Press through a mouli or potato ricer to remove the bits of bean skin.

Put about 4 tablespoons of the olive oil in a saucepan, add the sliced onion, and cook until soft and translucent. Add the chile and remaining garlic and cook for about 5 minutes

more. Add the tomatoes and puréed beans, plus salt and freshly ground black pepper. Cook for about 5 minutes, then add the leek, celery, thyme, potatoes, the remaining carrots, and cabbage. Bring to a boil and simmer until the vegetables are done—about 20 minutes.

Add the whole beans, season to taste, reheat, and serve immediately or set aside until the next day for ribollita.

To make the ribollita, first reheat the soup. Rub the toast with the garlic butter and put into 4 big bowls. Add the lettuce, ladle the soup over the top, and drizzle with a little olive oil. Sprinkle with parsley, then serve.

1½ cups dried cannellini beans

2 onions (1 cut in 4 wedges through the root, and 1 sliced)

3 carrots (1 cut into quarters lengthwise, and 2 sliced)

6 garlic cloves, smashed

6 tablespoons extra-virgin olive oil, plus extra for drizzling

1 fresh chile, seeded and sliced

2 cups tomatoes, peeled and chopped

1 leek, sliced

2 celery stalks, finely diced

sprigs of thyme

3 waxy potatoes, cubed

1 Savoy cabbage (or *cavalo nero*,) sliced

sea salt and freshly ground black pepper

ribollita

8 slices ciabatta bread, toasted

4 tablespoons butter, mashed with 1 crushed garlic clove

1 romaine lettuce, sliced

4 tablespoons chopped parsley (optional)

serves 4

There are many versions of the classic Caesar Salad—the archetypal meal for Ladies Who Lunch. The remarkable Julia

caesar salad

Child says anchovies weren't used in the original, but Worcestershire sauce was (and that contains anchovies.) It also included a one-minute egg, but like so many wonderful things, this would be regarded as unsafe these days, and I have included a soft-cooked 4-minute egg. I do love her recommendation for serving the leaves whole—dip them into the dressing and eat them with your fingers, then eat the croutons with a fork.

1 small head romaine lettuce

2 tablespoons extra-virgin olive oil

½ tablespoon lemon juice, plus 1 lemon, cut in wedges

sea salt flakes and freshly ground black pepper

croutons

1 thick slice challah bread, brioche, or other white bread

oil and/or butter, for sautéing

1 large garlic clove, smashed

to serve

3–4 rinsed anchovy fillets

1 soft-cooked (4-minute) medium-sized egg, peeled and halved or quartered

Parmesan cheese, shaved into curls with a vegetable peeler

serves 1

To make the croutons, toast the slice of bread or brioche lightly. Cut into big cubes, cutting off and discarding the crusts. Heat the oil and butter in a skillet and add the garlic clove. Add the cubes of bread and cook, turning, until golden on all sides. Discard the garlic after about 1 minute—do not let it burn. When the cubes are golden, remove and drain on kitchen paper.

Put the lettuce in a large bowl and sprinkle with olive oil. Using your hands, roll the leaves in the oil. Sprinkle with lemon juice and roll again.

Divide the croutons between 4 big bowls and put the dressed whole leaves on top. Sprinkle with salt and lots of freshly ground black pepper. Add the anchovies, egg, and shavings of Parmesan and serve.

Note: If you don't like anchovies, omit them, and add 1 teaspoon Worcestershire sauce to the dressing.

salads

blue cheese salad

with crispy pancetta and pignolis

This salad of herb sprigs and mixed leaves—peppery, soft, and bitter—is dressed with a creamy blue cheese dressing. It's suitable for an appetizer, a salad course after the meat, or as a big-bowl lunch, as here.

2 tablespoons pignoli nuts

1 tablespoon olive oil, for cooking

8–12 slices smoked pancetta

4 oz. Dolcellate, Gorgonzola, or other blue cheese, diced

3 tablespoons extra-virgin olive oil, or to taste

1 tablespoon white rice vinegar or lemon juice, or to taste

mixed salad leaves, including peppery leaves like watercress and mustard, bitter ones like frisée, soft ones like mignonette or butter lettuce, and herb sprigs like arugula

1 avocado, scooped into balls with a teaspoon (optional)

sea salt flakes and freshly ground black pepper

serves 4

Put the pignolis in a dry skillet and sauté for about 1 to 2 minutes only, until golden. Set aside.

Heat the olive oil in the skillet, add the pancetta, and sauté until crispy. Transfer to a plate lined with paper towels to drain.

Put the cheese in the bottom of a large salad bowl and crumble well with a fork. Add the extra-virgin olive oil and vinegar or lemon juice, Mash, then beat to a loose and creamy consistency. Add lots of freshly ground black pepper and salt to taste.

Put the salad leaves on top of the cheese dressing, then add the avocado, if using. Sprinkle with the pancetta and pignolis (scrape any crunchy bits from the skillet into the bowl too.)

Serve, in the salad bowl, for guests to help themselves, or make in 4 big bowls, dividing the ingredients as appropriate. Lots of wine and some crusty bread are the perfect accompaniments.

There are as many variations of this Tuscan bread salad as there are cooks.

panzanella

The trick is to let the flavors blend well without allowing the bread to disintegrate into a mush. The key is to use the ripest, reddest, most flavorful tomatoes you can find ("marmande" are my favorite.)

6 very ripe plum tomatoes

2 garlic cloves

4 thick slices day-old bread, preferably Italian-style

½ cucumber, halved, seeded, and finely sliced diagonally

1 red onion, diced

1 tablespoons chopped parsley

8–12 tablespoons extra-virgin olive oil

2 tablespoons white rice vinegar

1 teaspoon balsamic vinegar (optional)

1 bunch of basil leaves, torn

12 caperberries, or to taste (optional)

sea salt and freshly ground black pepper

serves 4

Cut the plum tomatoes in half, spike with slivers of garlic, and roast in the oven at 400°F for about 1 hour until wilted and some of the moisture has evaporated.

Meanwhile, tear the bread into pieces and put in a bowl. Sprinkle with a little water until damp. Add the tomatoes, cucumber, onion, parsley, salt, and pepper. Sprinkle with the olive oil and vinegar, toss well, then set aside for about 1 hour to develop the flavors. Add the basil and caperberries and serve.

Variation: Toast the slices of bread under the broiler or cook on a char-grill before tearing into pieces.

There is much debate about the correct ingredients for this salad. Some experts say all the vegetables should be raw, others not. Usually, canned tuna would be used, but modern cooks have improved upon what was already a perfect dish by char-grilling the tuna until rare. Another wonderful method is to stew it gently in olive oil for 30 to 45 minutes. Substitute as you like.

salade niçoise

1 lb. Chinese snake beans, green beans, or sugarsnap peas

4 oz. shelled fava beans

2 orange, red, or yellow bell peppers (optional)

1 thick slice fresh tuna, about 1 lb.

4 tablespoons extra-virgin olive oil, plus extra, for brushing

4 teaspoons white rice vinegar

mixed salad leaves, to taste

8 cherry tomatoes, halved

12–20 black Provençal olives

4 soft-boiled (4-minute) eggs (optional)

sprigs of basil (optional)

4–8 anchovy fillets, rinsed (optional)

salt and freshly ground black pepper

serves 4

If using snake beans, cut them in to 3-inch lengths. Cook the beans in boiling salted water until just al dente, then refresh in ice water. Pat dry.

Cook the fava beans in boiling salted water until tender. Cool quickly in ice water, then drain and pop them out of their gray skins. Prepare the bell peppers, if using (see note.)

Brush the tuna with 1 tablespoon olive oil, then char-grill on a stove-top grill-pan until crisp outside and pink inside. Remove and cut into ½-inch slices.

Divide the remaining oil, rice vinegar, salt, and pepper between 4 big bowls and beat with a fork. Add the salad leaves and toss well. Add the beans, tomatoes, olives, and tuna slices. Cut the eggs, if using, into quarters and add to the bowls. Top with basil and anchovy fillets, if using, sea salt flakes, and lots of freshly ground black pepper.

Note: To peel the peppers, char them over a flame or under the broiler. Scrape off the burned skin and slice the flesh. I love the taste of charred peppers, but it's not traditional. If serving raw peppers, I prefer to peel them with a vegetable peeler, then core and slice into strips—I think pepper skin is totally indigestible. (Red, yellow, or orange peppers only please!

1 cooked Chinese duck

1 pomelo

1 package beansprouts, trimmed then kept in ice water

8 tablespoons light olive oil (not extra-virgin)

3–4 tablespoons rice vinegar

2 teaspoons soy sauce

4 teaspoons Worcestershire sauce

8 oz. package mixed leaf salad

freshly ground black pepper

serves 4

These cold salad ingredients are served with warm duck. Buy a whole barbecued duck from Chinatown (don't let them chop it up), or use duck breasts as described in the variation. Pomelos can also be found in Chinese, Thai, or Vietnamese fruit shops. Like huge, dry-fleshed grapefruit, their segments stay together without losing their juice. If you can't find them, use a pink grapefruit instead. Eat this dish with chopsticks—the perfect salad-eating implements. In fact, they can be recommended for almost all salad-eating activities!

chinese duck salad
with pomelo and beansprouts

Slice the breasts off the duck in whole pieces. Put them, skin side down, on the work surface, then slice crosswise in 1-inch strips. Set aside. Remove the crispy skin from the remaining duck, and cut into pieces about 1 inch square. Set aside. Shred the remaining duck meat into pieces as large as possible.

Pull the skin off the pomelo, then pull the membranes off each segment with your fingers (don't worry if they break—each one should be broken into 2 or 3 pieces anyway.) Set aside. Drain the beansprouts.

Mix the olive oil, rice vinegar, soy sauce, pepper, and Worcestershire sauce together, then divide between 4 big bowls. Add the leaves and turn them 3 to 4 times in the dressing until evenly coated. Add a pile of beansprouts, some shredded meat, then some breast and crispy skin. Top with the pomelo and serve.

Variation: No Chinese duck? Instead, char-grill 4 duck breasts until crispy in a stove-stop grill-pan, then slice crosswise and proceed as in the main recipe. Alternatively, marinate overnight in ½ cup rice vinegar mixed with 2 tablespoons soy sauce, 2 tablespoons fish sauce (Thai nam pla or Vietnamese nuoc mam,) and 1 tablespoon chile oil, then char-grill.

Thai salads are incredibly easy to make, and absolutely packed with flavor. Don't worry if you can't find all these ingredients—ring the changes according to whatever's available. I've used shrimp, but you could use shredded barbecued pork, chicken, or duck breast, for example. Rice vermicelli is like fine spaghetti: rice sticks like strappy fettuccine. Obviously, increase quantities for more servings.

1 tablespoon sesame seeds

1 bundle rice sticks or vermicelli

sprigs of cilantro

your choice of

½ **nashi pear, sliced lengthwise**

½ **green mango or green papaya**

½ **baby cucumber**

1 **handful beansprouts, trimmed**

2 **fresh shiitake mushrooms**

1 **clump enokitake mushrooms**

3 **cherry tomatoes, halved**

3 **cooked jumbo shrimp, peeled**

1 **inch daikon (mooli), peeled and finely sliced**

chile dressing

1 **teaspoon chile oil**

1 **teaspoon fish sauce**

2 **teaspoons lime juice**

1 **teaspoon vegetable oil**

½ **teaspoon soy sauce**

½ **teaspoon sugar**

serves 1

thai noodle salad
with shiitakes and chile dressing

Stir-fry the sesame seeds in a dry skillet for 1 minute or until golden. Set aside. Mix the dressing ingredients together in a small bowl or screw-top jar.

Put the rice stick or vermicelli noodles in a bowl and cover with boiling water for 3 minutes for vermicelli, or 10 minutes for rice sticks. Drain, rinse in cold water, then drain again, return to the bowl, and cover with ice water and ice cubes. Drain just before serving.

Peel the mango or papaya with a vegetable peeler. Slice the flesh diagonally into strips. Cut the baby cucumber in half lengthwise and scoop out the seeds. Peel, leaving strips of green. Slice finely diagonally. Remove and discard the stems from the shiitakes and slice the caps crosswise into 4 to 6 pieces. Cut off and discard the roots from the enokitakes.

Tip the dressing into a big bowl, add the drained noodles, toss, then top with your choice of ingredients. Sprinkle with sesame seeds and cilantro, then serve.

Simmer the sauce ingredients in a saucepan for 5 minutes, then chill. Cook the noodles according to the package instructions, then drain, rinse in cold water, and cool quickly over ice. Chill.

Put the shiitakes in a saucepan, cover with 1 cup boiling water, and soak until soft. Remove and discard the mushroom stems. Add the soy sauce and mirin to the pan, bring to a boil, and simmer for a few minutes until the liquid is slightly reduced. Cool and chill.

Poach the shrimp in simmering salted water for about 1 minute until firm, then peel them, leaving the tail fins intact. Devein and split each shrimp down the back to the fin, giving a butterfly shape. Chill.

Put the noodles in a bowl. Add a few ice cubes and top with the shrimp, scallions, and mushrooms. Pour over the mushroom cooking liquid. Serve with separate dishes of wasabi paste and dipping sauce.

14 oz. soba noodles

12 dried shiitake mushrooms

2 tablespoons soy sauce

2 tablespoons mirin

12 uncooked shrimp

12 scallions, finely sliced

4 tablespoons wasabi paste

dipping sauce

1 cup dashi stock

½ cup Chinese rice wine or ginger wine

serves 4

Soba noodles are made from buckwheat. Firmer than other noodles, they are well suited to salad combinations. However other Japanese noodles are also delicious served cold. You could substitute white somen noodles, or the larger, ribbon-like udons. This salad is endlessly adaptable —you can omit the shrimp and use sliced chicken or duck breast, poached fish (fresh or smoked), and some salad leaves. Mirin is Chinese rice wine—if unavailable, the alternative usually recommended is dry sherry, but I rather like ginger wine, which is both sweet and spicy. Dashi stock is available as a powder or concentrate in Asian shops and larger supermarkets.

japanese iced soba noodle salad

fresh pasta dough

2 cups all-purpose flour

2 free-range eggs

2 free-range egg yolks

a pinch of salt

pesto and gorgonzola sauce

4 oz. Gorgonzola or Dolcellate cheese, chopped

½ cup milk

⅓ cup heavy cream

2 tablespoons butter

4 tablespoons pesto, plus extra, to serve

to serve

sprigs of basil

shavings of Parmesan cheese

sea salt and cracked black pepper

serves 4

> A sinful combination of two very rich pasta sauces —and absolutely delicious! Make your own fresh pasta if you have a machine, otherwise buy dried pasta and cook according to the package instructions.

fettuccine

with pesto and gorgonzola sauce

If making your own fresh pasta, put all the ingredients for the pasta dough into a food processor and work to a dough. Knead until the dough comes together, then roll through a pasta machine according to the manufacturer's instructions. Cut with the fettuccine attachment.

To make the sauce, melt the cheese in a saucepan with the milk, cream, and butter, and cook, stirring, until the sauce is thickened (about 5 minutes.*)

Cook the pasta in a large saucepan of salted water until al dente for dried pasta, or until it rises to the surface (about 1 to 2 minutes) for fresh pasta. Drain and divide between 4 big bowls. Spoon the sauce on top, then add an extra teaspoon of pesto and a sprig of basil to each one. Serve with the Parmesan shavings, some cracked pepper, and a small dish of sea salt.

*__Note:__ The pesto can be stirred into the sauce at this point, or spooned on top of the pasta just before serving.

rice and beans

Simmer the pumpkin and potato, if using, in a saucepan until tender. Drain and mash with half the butter until creamy—it should have the consistency of thick soup (add a little milk if necessary.)

Heat the oil and remaining butter in a skillet, add the onions, and sauté gently until soft and translucent. Add the garlic and cook until lightly golden (about 1 to 2 minutes.) Add the rice and stir-fry for 1 to 2 minutes until the grains are well-covered with oil. Add a quarter of the stock and simmer gently, stirring, until absorbed. Repeat until all the stock has been used and the risotto is creamy and fluffy. Stir the pumpkin through the risotto and serve, topped with the Parmesan, deep-fried pumpkin crisps, and chervil.

Note: To make pumpkin crisps, finely slice segments of pumpkin on a mandoline or with a vegetable peeler (include the skin.) Deep-fry in vegetable oil until crispy. Drain on paper towels.

1 lb. peeled and seeded pumpkin, cut into large chunks

4 potatoes, peeled and cut into large chunks (optional)

2 tablespoons butter

milk (optional—see method)

4 tablespoons olive oil

2 onions, finely chopped

2 fat garlic cloves, crushed

2 cups risotto rice

4 cups boiling chicken stock

to serve

shavings of Parmesan cheese

pumpkin crisps (see note)

sprigs of chervil (optional)

serves 4

A Pacific-Rim version of Risotto al Zucca. Pumpkin is a much-loved vegetable in Australia and New Zealand—roasted, puréed or souped. This is a variation on those cooking methods. As a pumpkin aficionado, I always use those with green or gray skins—they are drier and denser than the watery butternut kind, giving a more intense flavor and better texture.

pumpkin risotto

ful medames

with tabbouleh and egyptian flatbread

A simple, delicious Egyptian dish served as an appetizer or as a whole meal with wonderful Arab flatbreads: I like the huge ones, like giant pastry scarves. Hamine eggs are a traditional accompaniment—cooked for hours with onion skins, giving them an unusual color and texture. I prefer it without them, but a small side dish of quails' eggs is a happy compromise.

2 cups dried ful (fava beans)

8 scallions, sliced

2–4 garlic cloves, crushed

4 tablespoons olive oil

1 bunch of parsley, chopped

zest and juice of 1 lemon

sea salt and cracked pepper

tabbouleh

¾ cup toasted buckwheat

2 large ripe red tomatoes

1 bunch of flat-leaf parsley

1 large bunch of mint

3 scallions, sliced

2 tablespoons fruity olive oil

1 tablespoon lemon juice

sea salt and cracked pepper

to serve

sprigs of parsley

8 quails' eggs, boiled

Egyptian flatbread

serves 4

Soak the beans for 6 to 8 hours in cold water to cover. Drain the beans, put in a saucepan, cover with cold water, (do not salt,) bring to a boil, skim, then reduce to a simmer and cook for 1 hour or until tender (the time will depend on the age of the beans.) Drain. Meanwhile, put the garlic in a bowl, and mash with the oil, salt, and pepper. Add the beans and toss well in the garlicky oil (the garlic taste will soften a little in the heat.) Taste, and add extra sea salt and cracked pepper if needed. Fork through the chopped parsley and lemon juice and zest.

To make the tabbouleh, soak the buckwheat in water for 20 minutes, then drain. Peel, seed, and chop the tomatoes, and chop the parsley and mint. Put the tomatoes in a bowl with the buckwheat, chopped herbs, scallions, and cracked pepper. Sprinkle over the olive oil and lemon juice and toss well. Taste and adjust the seasoning.

To serve, put a large ladle of the ful medames in each of 4 big bowls, with a second large ladle of tabbouleh beside. Top with sprigs of parsley and lemon zest, then serve while the beans are still warm, together with large lacy Egyptian flatbreads and a dish of quails' eggs.

Variation: Ful medames and tabbouleh are delicious wrapped in the flatbread (sauced with hummus,) or in crisp romaine lettuce leaves.

tortellone
with walnut sauce

This walnut sauce is wonderful with pasta, and it echoes the filling of the tortellone (make your own — or buy homemade ones from a good Italian deli.) The sauce is very filling, so a little goes a long way — try it also as a stuffing for chicken breasts, or to top char-grilled steak.

To make the sauce, heat the oil in a small skillet, and sauté the garlic for about 1 minute until golden. Purée the walnuts, parsley, ricotta, cream, garlic, and olive oil in a food processor. Just before serving, transfer to a saucepan and cook, stirring, for a few minutes until well heated and slightly thinned, adding extra water if needed.

To make the tortellone, make the pasta dough according to the recipe on page 34. Mix the ricotta, Parmesan, spinach, basil, nutmeg, and seasonings in a bowl. Roll out the pasta dough, cut into circles around a small saucer, brush beaten egg around the edges, and put 1 to 2 tablespoons of the ricotta mixture in the center of each one. Fold over the pasta to make half circles, seal the edges, then turn them up like a hat brim and press the points together, sealing with more beaten egg.

Cook the tortellone in boiling salted water until they rise to the surface then cook 2 minutes more. Put 3 to 5 tortellone in each of 4 big bowls, top with the walnut sauce, and serve.

tortellone

⅔ cup ricotta cheese

4 tablespoons grated Parmesan cheese

½ cup cooked, chopped spinach

10 basil leaves, torn

¼ teaspoon ground nutmeg

sea salt and freshly ground black pepper

1 quantity fresh pasta dough (page 34)

1 egg yolk, beaten

walnut sauce

2 tablespoons olive oil

2 garlic cloves, sliced

1 cup fresh shelled walnuts, blanched and peeled*

2 cups chopped flat-leaf parsley

½ cup ricotta cheese

1 cup light cream or crème fraîche

salt and pepper

serves 4

*Note: The walnuts need not be blanched and peeled, but the flavor and color will be vastly improved if they are. It's a little time-consuming, but the peeled walnuts can be frozen until you're ready to cook them.

moroccan harira soup

with garbanzo beans and lentils

Though described as a soup, this filling dish of garbanzos is really a stew, and is used to break the fast of Ramadan. Though usually made with lamb, I have omitted it for a great vegetarian treat.

¾ **cup dried garbanzo beans (chickpeas)**

½ **cup yellow lentils or split peas (channa dhaal)**

2 **tablespoons sweet butter**

1 **tablespoon olive oil**

2 **onions, minced**

2 **garlic cloves, crushed**

1 **inch fresh ginger, minced**

1 **cinnamon stick**

1 **teaspoon ground turmeric**

2 **cups crushed tomatoes, or 2 lb. fresh tomatoes, peeled, seeded, and chopped**

juice of 1 lemon

sea salt and cracked pepper

2 **tablespoons beurre manié (optional)—see note**

to serve

torn cilantro leaves

8 **boiled quails' eggs (optional)**

serves 4

Soak the garbanzo beans for 6 to 8 hours in cold water to cover. Drain, put into a saucepan, cover with boiling (unsalted) water, and simmer until tender—about 1 hour, but the time will depend on the age of the beans. Drain (reserve the water to use in the dish if you like.)

Put the lentils or split peas in a saucepan, add 3 cups water, bring to a boil, reduce the heat, and simmer for 15 to 20 minutes.

Heat the butter and oil in a skillet, add the onions, and sauté until soft and translucent. Add the garlic, ginger, cinnamon, and turmeric and stir-fry for 5 minutes. Add 3 cups boiling water and simmer for 30 minutes. Add the lentils, garbanzo beans, and tomatoes to the skillet, stir well, then simmer for about 15 minutes to blend the flavors. Add the lemon juice and lots of cracked black pepper. Taste and adjust the seasoning with sea salt.

Serve in big bowls, sprinkled with cilantro leaves accompanied by a bowl of quails' eggs, if using.

Note: If necessary, you can thicken the sauce by stirring in 2 tablespoons beurre manié (1 tablespoon cornstarch mashed with 1 tablespoon butter.) Cook for a few minutes until thickened.

char-grilled shrimp
in chile-lemongrass marinade

Much of the flavor in prawns is in the shells, so cooking them unshelled releases the most marvellous flavor. In this Vietnamese-influenced dish, people peel their own prawns, so provide a big bowl for the debris and hot towels to help with the clean-ups. This is a hands-on dish!

Heat 1 tablespoon of the oil in a small skillet, add the garlic, and cook for 1 minute until golden. Transfer to a wide shallow dish, then stir in another 2 tablespoons of the oil, plus the next 9 ingredients.

Rinse the shrimp (not too long or you'll wash away the flavor.) Push a toothpick into the shrimp at the back of the neck, between the head and the shell, and carefully prise out the dark vein (it should come out in one piece.) Add the shrimp to the dish and turn to coat. Set aside to marinate for 30 minutes.

Heat a stove-top grill-pan, add the remaining oil, and heat again. Add the shrimp, in batches if necessary, and cook for about 3 to 5 minutes on each side until the shells turn red and the flesh becomes opaque all the way through (the time will depend on the size of the shrimp.)

Remove to heated bowls as they are ready. Serve with sprigs of cilantro and grated lime zest. The fish sauce, lime wedges, and a basket of hot towels should be served separately.

4 tablespoons corn or peanut oil

2 garlic cloves, crushed

6 red serrano chiles, very finely sliced

3 tablespoons fish sauce (*nam pla* or *nuoc mam*)

1 teaspoon salt

3 tablespoons rice vinegar

1 teaspoon sugar

6 kaffir lime leaves, finely sliced

3 stalks lemongrass, split lengthwise and finely chopped

1 large onion, finely chopped

juice of 3 limes

about 8–16 oz. whole uncooked shrimp per person

to serve

sprigs of cilantro

grated kaffir lime zest

fish sauce (Thai *nam pla* or Vietnamese *nuoc mam*)

lime wedges

serves 4

ultry and meat

bengali fish curry

on basmati coconut rice

Bengal is renowned as one of the culinary capitals of India, a country in which every state has its own distinctive regional style, each as different as, for instance, those of France and Italy. Bengal is known for its use of aromatic mustard oil as a cooking medium, especially for fish. If you can't find mustard oil (widely available in Asian markets) use corn oil and a little extra mustard seed to compensate. Don't use fine-flavored or soft-fleshed fish for this recipe—the spices mean that you need a strong-flavored, firm-fleshed fish like mackerel or cod.

1 teaspoon salt

2 teaspoons ground turmeric

2 lb. thick fish fillets, cut into pieces about 3–4 inches square

4 tablespoons mustard oil or corn oil

4 onions, cut in wedges through the root, separated into petals

1 tablespoon crushed garlic

1 inch fresh ginger, minced

1 mild chile, cored and sliced

6 cardamom pods, crushed

1 tablespoon mustard seeds

1 cup plain yogurt

1 cup coconut milk

basmati coconut rice

1 cup basmati rice, washed in several changes of water

1 teaspoon salt

2 tablespoons coconut milk

4 sprigs of cilantro, to serve

serves 4

Mix the salt and turmeric together and rub all over the fish. Heat the oil in a skillet or wok and sauté the fish for a few minutes on each side until almost cooked. Remove to a plate and keep them warm.

Add the onions and stir-fry gently until soft and translucent. Raise the heat and cook until lightly golden. Add the garlic and ginger and stir-fry until the garlic is cooked but not browned. Add the chile, cardamom, and mustard seeds. Stir-fry until the mustard seeds pop. Stir in the yogurt and coconut milk, and heat gently without boiling. Add the fish and simmer gently for about 5 minutes until the fish is cooked through.

Meanwhile, put the rice in a saucepan with the salt, coconut milk, and enough cold water to reach 1 finger's joint above the rice. Bring to a boil, put on the lid, reduce the heat, and cook at a gentle simmer for about 12 to 15 minutes until the water is absorbed and the rice fluffy. Turn off the heat and leave the pan covered for 15 minutes more.

Divide the rice between 4 big bowls and place the pieces of fish on top. Spoon over the sauce and garnish with a sprig of cilantro.

neapolitan seafood stew

A great dish with assertive flavors that remind me of wonderful holidays spent with my cousin in Naples. The fish market there has seafood so fresh it will bite you if you aren't careful, and the shellfish squirts water at you as you pass by. Alter the composition of this soup-stew according to what's available in your local market, but include thick white fish, shellfish, and crustacea such as shrimp.

4 large garlic cloves, crushed

1 bunch of thyme or rosemary

12 clams or other bivalves

12 mussels

about 4 tablespoons olive oil

2 large onions, cut into wedges through the root

8 ripe, very red tomatoes, peeled, halved, and seeded

2 lb. thick boneless white fish fillets, such as cod

4–8 small whole fish, cleaned and scaled (optional)

8 uncooked shrimp

4 cups boiling fish stock

sea salt and freshly ground black pepper

serves 4

Put 1 cup water in a saucepan with 1 crushed garlic clove and half the herbs, bring to a boil, then simmer to extract the flavors. Add the clams, cover with a lid, and cook at a high heat, shaking the pan from time to time. Remove them as they open (about 1 minute) and put on a plate so they don't overcook. Add the mussels, cover with a lid, and cook until they open. Remove as they do so and add to the clams. Taste the cooking stock and, if not too gritty, strain it through coffee filters into a cup and set aside.

Heat the oil in a large skillet, add the onion wedges, and cook until lightly browned on both sides. Reduce the heat and cook until softened. Stir in the remaining garlic and cook for a few minutes until golden. Add lots of freshly ground black pepper, then the tomatoes, remaining herbs, both kinds of fish, and the shrimp. Pour in the stock and heat just to boiling point. Reduce the heat and simmer for a few minutes until the fish turns opaque. Add the mussels, clams, and the strained mussel poaching liquid, if using. Reheat and season to taste.

Divide between 4 big bowls. Serve with crusty Italian bread and a pitcher of light red wine or the peppery white wine from the Vesuvius area on the Bay of Naples.

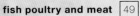

Put the duck, skin side down, on a stove-top grill-pan and cook at high heat until the fat begins to run. Reduce the heat to medium and add the sausages. Continue cooking, pouring off the fat from time to time, until the breast skin is crispy and the sausages are brown. Cook the other side, tipping off the fat from time to time.

Heat the oil in a flameproof casserole dish, add the garlic, and cook 1 minute until golden. Add the tomatoes, herbs, duck, and sausages, then enough stock just to cover the meat. Bring to a boil and simmer for about 35 minutes on top of the stove or in the oven. Remove the duck breasts and cut in ½-inch slices.

Cassoulets are perfect winter big bowl dishes. They always consist of beans and breadcrumbs baked with any number of meats. The traditional French dish from Toulouse should use a confit of goose or duck and the garlicky local sausage, but those I tasted in France went rather overboard on the beans and sausages. I felt a little cheated, so adapted the recipe for char-grilled duck breast. I think the traditional breadcrumbs taste like porridge and use an Italian gremolata instead. But if you would prefer the authentic taste, you can bake the dish topped with breadcrumbs.

Spread a layer of cooked beans over the bases of 4 ovenproof big bowls. Add a layer of sausages and sliced duck breasts, then an extra layer of beans to each. Boil down the stock until thickened, then pour into the big bowls, until the level of liquid is just below the top of the beans. Bake in a preheated oven at 400°F for 35 minutes or until crusty and light brown.*

Mix the gremolata ingredients together, sprinkle over the top of each bowl, and serve. A light salad is the only accompaniment you need.

***Note:** Alternatively, you can cook the cassoulet in a large casserole dish and serve in the big bowls.

2 large barbary duck breasts

4 coarse Italian pork sausages or Toulouse sausages

2 tablespoons olive oil

4 garlic cloves, crushed

1 cup crushed tomatoes

a bouquet garni of fresh thyme, bay leaves, and parsley

boiling chicken stock (see method)

dried haricot or butter beans, soaked 6–8 hours, then cooked without salt until tender

gremolata

4 tablespoons chopped parsley

1 garlic clove, crushed

grated rind of 1 lemon

serves 4

big bowl cassoulet
with char-grilled duck breasts and toulouse sausages

carbonade of beef
with mushrooms and mash

just made for the big bowl treatment. It's perfect with big flat field mushrooms thickly sliced and sautéed in butter or olive oil, plus lots of lovely mustard mashed potatoes to mop up the juices. The original recipe would use butter to cook the beef, but I prefer olive oil. Use either, or a mixture of both. It's also traditional to serve this dish with slices of fried toast, but I much prefer mashed potatoes—please yourself!

Cut the meat in large 2-inch cubes. Heat the olive oil in a flameproof casserole dish and brown the meat very well, in batches, removing them to a plate as they brown. Pour any juices into the dish of meat. Add the onions to the casserole (with a little more olive oil, if necessary) and cook gently until softened, translucent, and lightly browned. Add the garlic and stir-fry for a couple of minutes until golden. Push the garlic and onions to the side of the casserole with a slotted spoon. Sprinkle the flour over the oil in the pan and cook, stirring, until browned (make sure there aren't any white bits, or they will be lumps later.) Tip the meat and juices back into the pan, add the tomatoes, beer, and herbs, bring to a boil, reduce to a simmer, and cook, covered, on top of the stove or in a low oven for 2 to 3 hours.

Cool and chill, preferably overnight. One hour before serving, remove and discard the fat from the surface, then reheat gently on top of the stove or in the oven at 400°F.

Meanwhile, sauté the mushrooms in a little butter and oil and prepare the mashed potatoes. To serve, divide the mashed potatoes between 4 big bowls, spoon in the meat beside the potatoes, and top with the sautéed mushrooms.

Pour the hot stock carefully down the sides of the big bowls, then serve.

3 lb. braising beef

2–4 tablespoons olive oil

2 large onions, finely sliced

2 garlic cloves, crushed

2 tablespoons all-purpose flour

½ cup puréed tomatoes

2 cups Belgian-style beer (lager)

3 fresh bay leaves

1 bunch of thyme

sea salt and cracked pepper

to serve

sautéed mushrooms

creamy mashed potatoes

serves 4

lamb tagine

with honey and quinces

Fall quinces give wonderful scent to this Moroccan tagine. At other times of the year, you can substitute apples or even firm pears. I don't usually like honey or fruit with meat, but this tagine is an utterly delicious exception.

4 tablespoons olive oil

3 lb. lamb neck fillet, cut in big chunks (other cuts of meat will also work well)

2 onions, minced

3 tablespoons chopped parsley

1 inch fresh ginger, minced

1 cinnamon stick

1 pinch saffron threads, soaked in boiling water to cover for 20 minutes, or 2 sachets powder

2 quinces, 3 pears, or 3 apples, peeled, quartered, and cored

3 tablespoons honey

salt and pepper

sprigs of cilantro, to serve

pistachio couscous

2½ cups easy-cook couscous

5 cups boiling stock or water

4 tablespoons shelled pistachio nuts

2 tablespoons pignoli nuts

1 tablespoon butter

serves 4

Heat the olive oil in a flameproof casserole dish, add the meat, and sauté until browned. Add the onions, parsley, ginger, cinnamon, saffron, and enough boiling water to cover by about ½ inch. Return to a boil, skim, reduce to a bare simmer, and cook for about 1 hour, or until tender.

Remove the meat to a plate. Add the fruit, honey, salt, pepper, and 1 cup boiling water. Simmer until tender (a few minutes for pears and apples, longer for quinces, which will turn pink.)

Return the meat to the casserole dish, cover, and simmer for a further 15 minutes.

Meanwhile, put the couscous in a heatproof bowl, pour over boiling stock or water, and put in the oven to keep warm until all the liquid is absorbed. Blanch the pistachios and pop them out of their skins (so they're bright green.) Dry-toast the pignolis in a skillet until golden (about 30 seconds.) Stir the butter through the couscous, fluffing up the grains with a fork, then stir in the nuts.

Pile the couscous into the big bowls, spoon the tagine around, and top with sprigs of cilantro.

There is much discussion amongst aficionados about the precise composition of Irish stew. Some insist on carrots, others regard them as anathema. I like to use waxy yellow potatoes rather than the white floury kind, because they don't melt into the stock. The cloudy stock tastes wonderful, but I always think it looks a bit grim. This recipe keeps the stock clear and golden. I like to use big chunks of lamb, not the mimsy little bits you see in most recipes. That way the meat is much more succulent.

irish stew

Heat the oil or butter in a flameproof casserole dish and brown the onion wedges on both sides. Transfer to a plate, add the lamb to the pan, and sauté in batches until browned on all sides. Add the stock, wine, and seasoning. Bring to a boil, cover, reduce to a simmer, and cook for about 30 to 35 minutes. Remove from the heat, cool, and chill, preferably overnight.

2 tablespoons corn oil or butter

3 large onions, cut into 6 wedges through the root

3 lb. lamb neck fillet or similar stewing lamb, cut into large (about 2 inches) chunks

2¾ cups boiling chicken stock

1¼ cups white wine

2 lb. small waxy yellow potatoes, such as finger potatoes or Yukon gold, peeled

3 large carrots, sliced thickly, or 12 baby carrots

1 celery stalk, finely diced

beurre manié (1 tablespoon sweet butter mashed with 1 tablespoon all-purpose flour)—optional

1 bunch of parsley, chopped

sea salt and cracked pepper

serves 4

About 1 hour before serving, remove and discard the fat off the top, add the potatoes, carrots, and celery to the casserole, and simmer until the vegetables are tender. Stir in the beurre manié, if using, cook until lightly thickened, then taste and adjust the seasoning. To serve, divide between 4 big bowls, pour the stock over, sprinkle with parsley, and serve with chunks of soda bread and glasses of Guinness.

Variation:
scandinavian fishermen's stew

Interestingly—a stew made with beef, not fish. Perhaps the sailors get bored with fish! Substitute braising steak for the lamb, then remove it, and cook the onions in the same pan until soft and translucent. Thinly slice all the potatoes, put half in the base of a flameproof casserole dish, with the meat and onions on top. Add the remaining potatoes and seasoning. Pour 2¾ cups lager-style beer on top, bring to a boil, cover, and cook at a gentle simmer on top of the stove or in a low oven for about 1½ hours. Transfer the meat and vegetables to 4 big bowls, skim the fat off the pan juices, and pour the juice into the bowls. Serve with Danish beer and rye bread.

westphalian braised pork

with baby potatoes and smoked bacon

A deceptively simple recipe named for the former princely state of Westphalia on the North Sea coast of Germany—famous for the quality of its pork products. If the potatoes are very small, such as finger potatoes, leave them whole.

3 lb. small waxy potatoes, pink or yellow if possible, peeled and halved lengthwise if large

3 onions, cut into wedges through the root

about 8 slices smoked bacon (enough to cover the base of a casserole dish,) rinds removed

4 large or 8 small free-range pork chops

2¾ cups crème fraîche

½ cup white wine

½ cup white vermouth

1 cinnamon stick

4 tablespoons butter, diced

6 sprigs of thyme, plus extra, to serve

freshly ground black pepper

serves 4

Line the base of a flameproof casserole dish with slices of smoked bacon. Add a layer of the onions and potatoes, then arrange the pork chops on top. Pour in the crème fraîche, followed by the white wine and white vermouth. Tuck the cinnamon stick in the middle, then add a couple of large sprigs of thyme and lots of freshly ground black pepper.

Bring to a boil, immediately reduce the heat, cover with a lid, then simmer at the lowest possible heat (use a flame-tamer if necessary) for about 1 hour, or until the meat is falling off the bone. (Do not allow the liquid to boil, or the meat will be tough and the cream will separate.)

Transfer the meat to 4 big bowls, add a share of the bacon, onions, and potatoes, then strain the stock over the top. Add sprigs of thyme and serve.

If preferred, the pork can be sliced into bite-sized pieces and the dish served with a large soup spoon. Chunks of crusty French bread and a crisp white wine or lager are suitable accompaniments.

Vary the vegetables in this curry depending on what's good in the market, as a local cook would in Jamaica. Just try to avoid using butternut squash instead of real gray-or-green skinned pumpkin—it has rather watery flesh, and is a waste of time to a real pumpkin-lover! If you leave out the bacon, this curry is a gorgeous, spicy treat for vegetarians.

spicy caribbean vegetable curry
with crispy smoked bacon

2 tablespoons corn oil

4 slices smoked bacon or pancetta, snipped into strips (optional)

½ Scotch bonnet chile, seeded and sliced

1 cinnamon stick

3 cloves

6 green cardamom pods

1 red onion, cut into wedges through the root

2 cups chicken stock

2 cups coconut milk

boiled rice, to serve

your choice of

8 oz. pumpkin chunks

2 orange sweet potatoes, cut in chunks

1 plantain, peeled and sliced diagonally

1 choko (chayote), diced

8 round yellow eggplants

8 pattypan squash or 4 small zucchinis

1 cup sugarsnap peas

6 mini or 2 large red bell peppers, charred, peeled, and seeded

serves 4

Heat 1 tablespoon of the corn oil in a skillet, add the bacon or pancetta, if using, and cook until crispy. Remove from the skillet, drain on paper towels, and set aside.

Heat the remaining oil in the skillet, add the chile, cinnamon, cloves, and seeds from the cardamom pods, and stir-fry until you cough—that means the flavors have been released. Add the onion wedges and cook until well softened and slightly browned. Turn and cook the other side. Remove and set aside.

Add your choice of the pumpkin, sweet potatoes, plantain, choko, or eggplants and turn until well coated with the spices. Add the stock and cook until almost done. Add the pattypans or zucchinis, if using, and cook for 2 minutes. Add the sugarsnaps and cook for another 2 minutes. Pour in the coconut milk and bring to just below boiling (take care or the milk will split.) Add the prepared mini red bell peppers, if using, and the reserved onions, cover with a lid, and remove from the heat.

Divide the rice between 4 heated big bowls, add the vegetables and sauce, and top with the crispy bacon, if using.

This traditional sweet-but-savoury Thai concoction is amazingly easy to construct, and its garnishes can be added or subtracted according to whatever interesting ingredients you have to hand. However, there are a few you simply must have: cilantro, a chile or two, scallions, and a Thai curry paste—this one is the milder orange mussaman (Muslim) paste.

crisp thai noodles

with chiles, pork, and shrimp

4 bundles rice vermicelli noodles

corn oil, for deep-frying

garnishes

1 tablespoon corn oil

1 tablespoon Thai chile paste, such as mussaman

4 pork chops, boned and sliced

4–8 uncooked shrimp, peeled and split lengthwise if large

1–4 chiles, finely sliced

8 scallions, finely sliced

1 bunch of cilantro

sweet thai sauce

½ cup rice vinegar

½ cup palm sugar or dark brown sugar

4 tablespoons soy sauce

4 tablespoons fish sauce

serves 4

To make the sauce, put the vinegar, sugar, soy, and fish sauce in a small pan and cook, stirring until dissolved. Set aside to keep warm.

To prepare the garnishes, heat the oil in a skillet, add the Thai chile paste, and cook until you cough (about 1 to 2 minutes.) Add the pork strips and stir-fry until crispy. Add the shrimp and stir-fry for 1 minute. Transfer to a dish and keep them warm. Stir-fry the chiles and scallions for 1 minute, then add to the shrimp and pork.

To prepare the noodles, line 4 heated big bowls with crumpled paper towels, then fill a wok one-third full of corn oil and heat over a high heat to 375°F. To test, drop a fragment of noodle into the oil: the oil is hot enough when the noodle immediately puffs and curls. Add a bundle of noodles—they will puff up immediately. Let cook for 1 minute or until very pale gold then, using tongs, carefully turn the bundle over and cook the other side. Remove the noodles and put in one of the bowls. Repeat with the other 3 bundles (take care to reheat the oil and skim off any debris between batches.)

When all bundles are cooked, turn them over in the bowls and discard the paper. Put the pork, shrimp, scallions, and chiles on top of the noodles. Pour over the sweet hot dressing, and top with cilantro sprigs. Serve immediately with chopsticks.

index